Her Healing Season

Her Healing Season

Dr. Fallon McIver

Her Healing Season

Copyright © 2025, by Dr, Fallon McIver

ISBN: 979-8-9996343-2-0

Published by: The Chosen Pen Group

Printed in the United States of America

DEDICATION

Sis, if you're holding this book, it's not by accident. You didn't just stumble on it while scrolling online or walking past it in a store. No, this landed in your hands because God heard your silent prayers, saw your tears, and decided it's time.

Time for healing.

Time for release.

Time for you.

ACKNOWLEDGEMENTS

My daughter, if you ever read this, I pray you see my heart, my flaws, my growth, and my love for you in these words. I pray you know that even in my unhealed moments, my love for you never wavered.

My son, you've been my anchor in storms that you didn't even know were raging. I pray you always see the strength God put in your mama, and that it inspires you to honor and protect the women in your life.

For my man, my A1 since day 1, thank you for loving me with patience, intention, and consistency. You've been a safe place I didn't know I needed, and a reflection of the kind of love God always meant for me. You remind me daily that real love doesn't rush, doesn't harm, and doesn't hide.

CONTENTS

INTRODUCTION

Pull up a chair, Sis… let's talk.

Before we dive into these pages, I need you to know something: I didn't write from a place of "having it all together." I wrote this book from the trenches. Some of these pages were birthed with tears on my keyboard and prayers I didn't even have words for.

I was the little girl who learned too early how to survive in a house that didn't feel safe.

I've been the woman who carried that same little girl's wounds into relationships, trying to love my way into being loved back.

I've been the wife who stayed too long in something that was slowly killing me physically, emotionally, and spiritually because I thought that was what "honoring God" meant.

I've been the mother trying to raise children to be whole, while I was still bleeding from my unhealed cuts.

And, I've been the public servant, the leader, the one who could pour into hundreds yet go home empty.

This book is for the me in every woman reading. I wrote *Her Healing Season* for every woman who's ever had to smile in public while bleeding in private. For those who learned to hold it together because falling apart wasn't an option. I wrote for the ones who kept showing up for everybody else while wondering if anyone would ever show up for them.

This is for my sisters who are tired of the cycles, the secrets, and the silence. Tired of pretending that what happened to you didn't shape you. Tired of feeling like the little girl inside you never really got to grow up because she was too busy surviving.

I know you.

I see you.

I am you.

To my fellow daughters of dysfunctional families — the ones who've been pitted against siblings, gaslit by parents, silenced by "keep family business in the family" rules, I need you to know: You are not crazy. You are not unlovable. You are not broken beyond repair.

To the women who've carried childhood wounds into adulthood, those who've found themselves in marriages, relationships, and friendships that mirrored that same pain, I'm here to tell you that God has more for you. Healing is not only possible, it's your inheritance.

For every woman holding this book, I'm standing with you. Let's walk through this season together.

This is Her Healing Season.

And sis… it's your time.

We're going to talk about the real stuff: the dysfunctional families that make you second-guess your worth, the marriages that look good in pictures but are pure hell behind closed doors, the silent estrangements that break your heart but save your sanity, and the faith that somehow carried you even when you didn't know how to pray anymore.

We're going to unpack weight you've been carrying so long you forgot wasn't yours to carry in the first place. And we're going to make space for something new — peace, wholeness, and joy that isn't tied to other people's behavior.

Let me tell you this, God didn't just bring me through to leave me empty. He's restored my faith in love, in friendship, and in the power of a real support system. Somewhere along the way, He sent me a patient, deliberate, intentional man who loves me without trying to control me. One who sees my scars but doesn't treat me like I'm fragile. A man who lets me exhale. Sis, let me be clear, that part came after the healing started. You can't skip the work and expect the blessing to last.

Some days will sting. Others will feel like freedom. But each day, you'll get a scripture to anchor you, my story to walk with you, and space to write your own truth.

Here's what we're going to do. Over the next 33 days we'll walk through scriptures, stories, and straight-talk commentary. Each day, you'll have space to journal, reflect, and take action. We will start with Day 0, because I like to be different. By the end, you won't just have read a devotional, you'll have written pieces of your healing story. Grab your pen, open your heart, and let's get to it.

Because sis… it's your healing season.

— Dr. B

Day 0

The LORD is close to the brokenhearted;

he rescues those whose spirits are crushed.

Psalm 34:18 (NLT)

This is your season, Sis.

Not the "new year, new me" kind of season. I'm talking about the season where you finally get honest with yourself, pull up the roots that were killing you silently, and let God water the soil for something better.

Hey Sis, I'm Dr. B.

Before you flip through these pages thinking this is going to be a perfectly packaged, Instagram-filtered version of healing, let me stop you right there. This is raw. This is real. This is me with no makeup, no mask, and sometimes no chill. I'm about to pour you the kind of tea that might make you clutch your pearls and say, "Whew, she went there."

I wrote *Her Healing Season* because for too many years, I suffered in silence. My earliest wounds weren't from a man, they were from my own bloodline. A mother who never showed the love I craved.

A home where tension could be cut with a knife.

A father who was my safe place; the epitome of a servant, pastor, and protector who was taken from me by cancer when I was 17. From that moment, I felt like the only person who loved me unconditionally was gone; until I became a mother myself.

But life didn't stop throwing blows. Dysfunction followed me into adulthood, shaped the men I chose, and even slipped into my parenting. I stayed in a marriage 20 years too long because I thought honoring my late father's belief in "no divorce" was more important than honoring my own safety, sanity, and soul. That marriage? Abusive. Full of infidelity. And yet I tried to "fix" it until God stepped in and shut the door so hard, I couldn't reopen it if I tried.

My healing has been messy. I've made mistakes. I've provoked my children in my own unhealed moments. I've lost friends, cut off toxic family members, and been labeled "the angry Black woman" just for advocating for social justice and basic civility. And yet . . . I'm still here. Standing. Serving. Leading. Loving.

Sis, this book isn't me preaching at you from a mountaintop. It's me sitting across from you, coffee in hand, saying, *"Girl, I know exactly what you're feeling. Here's how I made it through."*

And yes, we're going to talk about the good stuff too. The man who's been my A1 since day 1, the dates that reminded me I was desirable, the self-care that kept me sane, and the moments God sent the exact people I needed, both personally and professionally, to heal wounds I didn't even know I still had.

This isn't just about surviving, Sis. This is about reclaiming the woman God designed before the pain, before the labels, before the betrayal.

Father,

Thank You for seeing me — the real me — even when I've been hidden under pain, shame, or survival mode. Thank You for bringing me to this moment where I can finally start to heal.

Guide me as I walk through these next 33 days with honesty, courage, and an open heart. Remind me that I'm not alone and that every broken piece is in Your hands.

In Jesus' name,

Amen.

Reflection / Call to Action:

One wound from my past that still feels unhealed? Write it down — no filter.

_____

_____

_____

_____

_____

When I think of "healing?" what is the first emotion that comes up for me?

_____

_____

_____

_____

_____

A short prayer asking God to meet me in this exact place:

_____

_____

_____

_____

_____

_____

_____

_____

_____

_____

_____

_____

_____

_____

Day 1

The Little Girl in Me

"Even if my father and mother abandon me, the Lord

will hold me close."

Psalm 27:10 (NLT)

Sometimes the deepest wounds start at home, long before we know how to name them.

Who was your safe person growing up? And what happens when the one place that should feel safe doesn't? For me, love often felt conditional. Approval was fleeting. My mother often forced me and my sibling into competition with each other. Because of that, comfort was scarce. An exception to that discomfort was my father. He was my safe place, my protector, and my biggest supporter. His presence was proof that unconditional love was possible, even in the midst of dysfunction.

Sis, if you grew up in chaos, I see you. You're not crazy, and you're not alone. That little girl in you still deserves to be safe, loved, and held; not by people who keep hurting her, but by the God who never leaves.

Lord,

Heal the little girl in me who still aches for love. Teach me to mother myself with compassion and truth. Hold me close and remind me that in You, I am fully loved and fully safe.

Amen.

Reflection / Call to Action:

Who was my safe person growing up?

_____

_____

_____

_____

_____

What truth does the little girl in me still need to hear today?

_____

_____

_____

_____

This is a letter to my younger self. Tell her she's safe now, and tell her who God says she is.

_____

_____

_____

_____

_____

_____

_____

_____

_____

_____

_____

_____

_____

Day 2

Sibling Rivalries, Generational Curses

"You intended to harm me, but God intended it all for good."

Genesis 50:20 (NLT)

Some of the deepest wounds don't come from strangers — they come from family.

Sis, have you ever noticed how family dynamics can follow you like a shadow? Generational dysfunction has a way of showing up again and again until someone says, "It stops here."

In my life, my brother absorbed the wedge created by my mother's favoritism, and it never really went away. His issue with me bled into adulthood and even trickled into my relationship with my daughter. They played both sides of the fence, and it created fractures that hurt more deeply than I could have imagined.

It's a hard truth: the ones closest to you can sometimes be the quickest to wound you. But here's the hope, God always provides covering. In my case, He gave me surrogate brothers who love, cover, and support me in ways my biological brother never did. God reminded me through them that blood may define family, but love defines brotherhood.

Father,

Break the generational curses that linger in my family line. Heal the fractures created in childhood, and replace dysfunction with love and truth. Surround me with people who cover me in ways blood relatives sometimes can't.

Amen.

Reflection / Call to Action:

Where have I seen cycles of dysfunction repeat in my family?

_____

_____

_____

_____

_____

What boundary do I need to set to protect my peace?

_____

_____

_____

_____

_____

Write a declaration renouncing one generational curse and replacing it with God's promise.

_____

_____

_____

_____

_____

_____

_____

_____

_____

_____

_____

_____

_____

_____

_____

_____

Day 3

When Loss Shapes You

"The Lord is close to the brokenhearted; he rescues those whose

spirits are crushed."

Psalm 34:18 (NLT)

Grief doesn't just leave a hole — it reshapes the way you love and trust.

Sis, grief changes everything. When someone you depend on is gone, the world feels unsteady, and the ripple effects show up in ways you don't always recognize. When my father passed away when I was 17, my world tilted. The one person who loved me unconditionally was gone, and that loss planted a deep vulnerability. I craved stability so badly that I settled for unhealthy love just to fill the void.

It shaped the way I mothered — shielding my children from chaos, sometimes through silence that created new wounds. My grief also revealed something sacred: when people leave, God remains. The Lord really is close to the brokenhearted. I didn't see it then, but He was carrying me all along.

Lord,

Heal the broken places grief has left in me. Thank You for being the Father who never leaves, the protector who never dies, and the anchor grief cannot take away.

Amen.

Reflection / Call to Action:

How has grief shaped the way I enter relationships?

_____

_____

_____

_____

_____

Where do I still feel the ache of loss?

_____

_____

_____

_____

_____

A prayer thanking God for carrying me in my grief:

_____

_____

_____

_____

_____

_____

_____

_____

_____

_____

_____

_____

_____

Day 4

When Silence Becomes Agreement

"Trust in the Lord with all your heart;

do not depend on your own understanding."

Proverbs 3:5 (NLT)

Sometimes the loudest mistake we make is in what we never ask God.

Have you ever moved forward without asking God's direction? Sometimes we assume love, timing, or potential is enough, but assumptions can become prisons.

For years, I never stopped to ask God if my ex-husband was meant to be my husband. I stayed in the marriage because tradition said marriage is forever. My father was a pastor and he didn't believe in divorce. I thought silence was strength, but silence in prayer left me blind. Silence in action left me stuck. By not inviting God into the choice, I handed the pen of my story to someone else.

Sis, don't confuse silence with strength. God isn't afraid of your questions. Seek Him first, and He'll show you what love, covenant, and freedom are supposed to look like.

Lord,

Forgive me for the times I moved without Your counsel. Teach me to seek You first, not last. Give me the courage to listen and obey, even when it goes against tradition, pressure, or fear.

Amen.

Reflection / Call to Action:

Where might silence be keeping me stuck?

_____

_____

_____

_____

_____

In what area of my life do I need God's clarity right now?

_____

_____

_____

_____

_____

What specific question I will bring to God this week, and how will I create space to listen for His answer?

_____

_____

_____

_____

_____

_____

_____

_____

_____

_____

_____

_____

_____

_____

_____

Day 5

The Final Straw

"You will know the truth, and the truth will set you free." John 8:32 (NLT)

Sometimes God allows one moment to break what should have been broken long ago.

Has someone's words ever cut so deep that they shifted your entire perspective?

For weeks, I had agreed to remain separated from my ex-husband instead of finalizing the divorce. Part of me was still clinging—maybe for the kids, maybe for tradition, maybe out of fear.

Then came the moment I'll never forget. My ex looked at everything I had worked for: my degrees, my leadership, my service to the community, and dismissed it all in one cruel statement. He said none of it was about purpose or calling. From his perspective, I only did it to prove to my mother that she chose the wrong child to favor, and that I wanted to live up to the expectations of my father who is no longer living.

That wasn't just an insult, it was a dagger to the very core of my identity and calling. It was an attempt to reduce my God-given purpose to pettiness and comparison. And in that moment, something in me broke free. Separation wasn't enough anymore. I knew I had to walk away for good.

Sis, sometimes God will use even the harshest words to snap the chains you've been too afraid to break. Painful as they are, those moments of truth can be the very doorway to freedom.

Father,

Thank You for exposing lies, even when they come through the mouths of others. Thank You for turning words meant to destroy me into the very spark that set me free. Give me courage to keep walking in Your truth, no matter the cost.

Amen.

Reflection / Call to Action:

A moment when someone's words opened my eyes.

What was said, and how did it impact me?

_____

_____

_____

_____

_____

What truth have I been avoiding because it hurts too much to face?

_____

_____

_____

_____

_____

A prayer to help me embrace freedom, even when it comes wrapped in painful clarity.

_____

_____

_____

_____

_____

_____

_____

_____

_____

_____

_____

_____

_____

_____

_____

Day 6

Answering God's Way Out

"The Lord himself will fight for you. Just stay calm."

Exodus 14:14 (NLT)

Bondage is when someone doesn't love you but still refuses to release you.

Sis, there's a dangerous kind of control where it's not about love — it's about power. That's where I found myself. My ex knew I held tightly to my father's conviction that divorce was never an option, and he used it against me. But I believe my daddy would've made an exception for a marriage full of lies, infidelity, and abuse. That was never God's covenant.

One night, I finally prayed: "Lord, if You want me to stay, I will. But if You want me to go, do it in such a way that I'll never come back." That prayer changed everything. Soon after, the door didn't just close — it slammed. I had to seek a domestic violence protective order. Painful, yes, but it was the clarity I begged for.

Even then, my ex tried one last jab: he wanted me to believe I was trapped. But what he didn't count on was the God who fights for His daughters.

Lord,

Thank You for shutting doors I was too weak to
close. Thank You for protecting me when I couldn't
protect myself. Give me courage to obey quickly when
You say, "move."

Amen.

Reflection / Call to Action:

Where have I confused control with commitment in my life?

_____

_____

_____

_____

_____

What doors has God closed that I'm trying to reopen?

_____

_____

_____

_____

_____

A prayer of surrender asking God to remove anything

not meant for me:

_____

_____

_____

_____

_____

_____

_____

_____

_____

_____

_____

_____

_____

_____

_____

Day 7

God's Provision Beyond Control

"And my God will supply all your needs from his glorious riches, which have been given to us in Christ Jesus."

Philippians 4:19 (NLT)

What feels like loss can actually be God making room for provision.

Sis, the enemy will try to convince you that leaving means losing everything. But God will always remind you that His supply doesn't depend on man's approval.

When I left, my ex told me flat out, "You know you can't afford to live anywhere else." And to be fair, I was still paying half the bills for a house I no longer lived in — because protecting my credit mattered to me. He counted on that being the chain that would keep me tied.

But what he didn't count on was God.

Friends opened their homes. A board member offered me a condo for a week so I could breathe and regain a sense of normalcy. Danny welcomed me in. Kelly said, "You can stay here forever." And not one of them charged me a dime.

That's the difference between man's control and God's care. My ex tried to weaponize money, but God showed me I would never lack. And here's the testimony — eventually, I even got my house back. That's the kind of full-circle provision only He can write.

Sis, let me sip you some tea: when people try to scare you with "you can't," God shows up with, "Watch Me."

Lord,

Thank You that Your provision outlasts every attempt to control me. Teach me to expect supply, not lack, when I trust You.

Amen.

Reflection / Call to Action:

Where have I mistaken loss for lack?

_____

_____

_____

_____

_____

How has God shown up in unexpected ways to provide

for me?

_____

_____

_____

_____

_____

What is one place in my life where I'm trusting Him to supply next?

_____

_____

_____

_____

_____

_____

_____

_____

_____

_____

_____

_____

_____

_____

Day 8

Rebuilding Strength & Peace

"He gives power to the weak and strength to the

powerless."

Isaiah 40:29 (NLT)

Freedom is one battle. Rebuilding and protecting your peace is the next.

Sis, getting out is one thing. Learning to breathe again is another.

When I got my house back, it felt like victory but the locks changing didn't erase the trauma. Silence doesn't automatically equal peace. I had to relearn myself: trusting my instincts, making choices without second-guessing, remembering I wasn't trapped anymore.

That quiet felt foreign at first, but then I realized: "this is peace." Not fake peace. Not quiet chaos. But real, soul-settling peace. Strength came with it. Every small step forward reminded me I wasn't a victim anymore; I was a survivor. Survivors become thrivers when they lean into God's strength, not their own.

Lord,

Thank You for peace that settles my spirit and strength that sustains me daily. Help me to guard both fiercely.

Amen.

Reflection / Call to Action:

Where do I need God's strength right now?

_____

_____

_____

_____

_____

What noise have I mistaken for normal that He's calling

me to release?

_____

_____

_____

_____

_____

A prayer for one small step forward I've made and I thank

Him for it:

_____

_____

_____

_____

_____

_____

_____

_____

_____

_____

_____

_____

_____

_____

Day 9

Purpose in the Pain

"And we know that God causes everything to work together for the good of those who love God and are called according to his purpose."

Romans 8:28 (NLT)

Pain doesn't cancel purpose. Sometimes, it sharpens it.

One of the wildest parts of my story is this: while my personal life was crumbling, God was elevating me in my calling. I was leading, serving, and showing up for my community, even when I felt shattered at home.

There were days I cried in the car, then walked into a boardroom with a smile. Some people called it strength. Truth? It was survival. Purpose wouldn't let me quit, even when my circumstances gave me every reason to. I often asked God, "How can You still use me when I'm this hurt?" But now I see, it was His reminder that my worth wasn't tied to a man, a marriage, or even my mistakes. My calling didn't end just because my marriage did.

Sis, let me give you the tea—purpose doesn't pause for pain. Sometimes God lets you serve even while you're bleeding, not because He wants you broken, but because He knows healing is already in motion. He will hold you together long enough for your assignment, and by the time you look back, you'll realize you were stronger than you thought.

Lord,

Thank You for reminding me that pain does not disqualify purpose. Strengthen me to keep walking in my calling even when life feels heavy. Let my scars testify that You can still bring beauty out of brokenness.

Amen.

Reflection / Call to Action:

When have I felt unqualified to lead or serve because of personal struggles?

_____

_____

_____

_____

_____

How has God reminded me that my calling is bigger than my circumstances?

_____

_____

_____

_____

_____

One way I can keep walking in purpose this week, even if

I feel weary:

_____

_____

_____

_____

_____

_____

_____

_____

_____

_____

_____

_____

_____

_____

Day 10

When Peace Becomes Your Clapback

"You will keep in perfect peace all who trust in you,

all whose thoughts are fixed on you!"

Isaiah 26:3 (NLT)

Sis, peace is the loudest response you'll ever give.

Let me keep it real. There was a time when every lie, whisper, and sideways look had me ready to defend myself. I rehearsed arguments in my head, wrote paragraphs I'd never send, tried to prove I wasn't who they painted me to be. But then God gave me something they couldn't touch—peace. That shift was wild. The same mess had knocked me off balance couldn't get a rise out of me anymore.

Here's the tea: nothing irritates people more than when the chaos they try to stir up doesn't move you. When they expect tears, you're smiling. When they expect you to fold, you're thriving. When they bring up your past, you're already living in your next chapter. That's God. That's growth. That's peace speaking louder than pain ever could.

Sis, stop wasting your breath trying to explain yourself to people committed to misunderstanding you. Sometimes the best clapback is no clapback at all—just peace, joy, and glowing in front of the same ones who tried to dim your light.

Lord,

Thank You for making my peace louder than the noise around me. Help me to stay steady in You when others try to pull me into drama. Let my calm be the proof that You're fighting battles I don't have to.

Amen.

Reflection / Call to Action:

What situation am I being called to let peace, not words, handle?

_____

_____

_____

_____

_____

How can I protect my energy when people try to bait me into old battles?

_____

_____

_____

_____

_____

One place in life where see I peace growing .A prayer to thank God for it:

_____

_____

_____

_____

_____

_____

_____

_____

_____

_____

_____

_____

_____

_____

x

Day 11

When Silence Turns to Beauty

"There is a time to be quiet and a time to speak."

Ecclesiastes 3:7 (NLT)

When God says, "speak," silence breaks and beauty begins.

Sis, for years I thought silence was strength. I stayed quiet about chaos, disrespect, and manipulation. I smiled in public and suffered in private, convincing myself that silence was dignity. But here's what I learned: silence has a season. And when that season is up, staying quiet keeps you bound. While I stayed silent, lies got loud. People filled in the blanks with their own stories about me. And my silence gave their voices more power than my truth.

Then God reminded me: there is a time to be quiet, and a time to speak. Breaking my silence wasn't about revenge—it was about release. It was about choosing freedom over fear, healing over hiding.

And here's the beauty: when I opened my mouth, God opened His hand. The ashes of my silence became seeds for something new. My shame turned into testimony. My mourning turned into joy. Just like Isaiah promised, He gave me beauty for ashes, joy for mourning, and praise for despair.

Sis, don't miss this: when you speak in God's timing, He doesn't just give you words, He gives you freedom and that freedom is beautiful.

Lord,

Thank You for teaching me the power of timing.
Give me courage to speak when silence no longer serves
You, and faith to trust that my words will be met with
Your beauty, not my shame.

Amen.

Reflection / Call to Action:

Where has silence protected me, and where has it kept me bound?

_____

_____

_____

_____

_____

What truth am I holding that God may be nudging me to release?

_____

_____

_____

_____

_____

A prayer asking God to exchange my silence for His

beauty, in His perfect timing:

_____

_____

_____

_____

_____

_____

_____

_____

_____

_____

_____

_____

_____

_____

_____

Day 12

Breaking the Cycle

"You will know the truth, and the truth will set you free."

John 8:32 (NLT)

Freedom starts when you call a thing what it is.

Sis, let me be real, cycles don't break by accident. They break when you stop pretending, stop minimizing, and start naming dysfunction for exactly what it is.

For me, the cycle started long before my marriage. My mother taught me early what favoritism felt like when she pitted me against my brother. He was always her golden child. That seed of division never left us; my brother carried it into adulthood, his family mirrored the same behavior, and eventually, those fractures bled into my household. The result? My daughter, my own flesh and blood, was caught in the middle of his games, and it helped break one of the bonds that should've been unshakable.

That's how generational dysfunction works. It doesn't die with the last person—it mutates. It shifts faces, but it keeps recycling the same pain until somebody says: "It stops here."

For years, I told myself staying quiet was "keeping the peace." But silence is not peace—it's permission. And the enemy thrives in silence, because what you won't confront, you unconsciously protect.

The turning point for me was finally saying out loud, "This is dysfunction. This is not normal. This is not love." And once I named it, I stripped it of its power.

Sis, don't let anyone gaslight you into believing you're "disrespectful" or "the problem" for telling the truth. Truth is not rebellion. Truth is deliverance. And sometimes your boldness to name it is the very key that frees not only you—but the generations after you.

Lord,

Give me the courage to name and confront the dysfunction that has lingered in my family for too long. Break every cycle of silence, favoritism, and manipulation. Heal the fractures, restore what the enemy tried to destroy, and let truth and freedom be the inheritance I leave behind.

Amen.

Reflection / Call to Action:

What dysfunction have I been calling "normal" just to survive?

_____

_____

_____

_____

_____

Who has benefitted most from my silence?

_____

_____

_____

_____

_____

A prayer for one generational curse I refuse to pass down. (Replace it with a scripture of promise and declare it over my life today).

_____

_____

_____

_____

_____

_____

_____

_____

_____

_____

_____

_____

_____

_____

Day 13

Breaking Family Fractures

"He heals the brokenhearted and bandages their wounds."

Psalm 147:3 (NLT)

Family can wound the deepest—but God can heal the deepest.

Sis, sometimes the heaviest pain doesn't come from outside, it comes from within your own bloodline. Strangers may hurt you, but family fractures cut to the bone. And when those fractures stretch across generations, it can feel like you're carrying pain older than you are.

The truth is, dysfunction doesn't always look loud—it can be subtle. It hides in favoritism, in unspoken competition, in the silence that says more than words ever could. One generation's rejection becomes the next generation's mistrust. And the cycle spins until someone finally says, "It stops here."

That's the beauty of God's healing. He doesn't just cover wounds, He restores lineages. Your courage to face the pain, your prayers over your children, and your refusal to carry silence forward are holy seeds that break curses. Seeds that shift bloodlines. Seeds that will outlive you.

So Sis, release the shame of what your family didn't get right. You don't heal by hiding fractures—you heal by handing them to the One who makes all things new.

Lord,

Heal every fracture in my family. End cycles of rejection, comparison, and division. Let love, grace, and truth flow through me so my children inherit freedom instead of dysfunction.

Amen.

Reflection / Call to Action:

What fracture in my family still weighs heavy on my

heart?

_____

_____

_____

_____

_____

A cycle you refuse to pass down:

_____

_____

_____

_____

_____

A prayer for God to plant something new in my family

line—starting with me:

_____

_____

_____

_____

_____

_____

_____

_____

_____

_____

_____

_____

_____

_____

Day 14

Choosing Freedom Over Familiarity

"So if the Son sets you free, you are truly free."

John 8:36 (NLT)

Just because it's familiar doesn't mean it's healthy.

Sis, cycles don't just live in people—they live in patterns. And the hardest part of healing is realizing how often dysfunction is mistaken for "normal." What you grew up around, what you tolerated in silence, and what you kept excusing—all of it can feel like home, even when it's breaking you.

But here's the truth: freedom requires new choices. You can't walk in healing while holding onto old habits. You can't pray for restoration while clinging to what God is trying to release. At some point, you have to look at what's "familiar" and admit: this is not serving me, this is not God's best, this stops with me.

And Sis, choosing freedom may feel lonely at first. People invested in the cycle won't clap for your breakaway. They'll call you "different, "distant", or even "wrong." But peace will prove you right. God will back you up every single time you choose His freedom over familiar chains.

Lord,

Give me the courage to walk away from what's familiar but unhealthy. Break every chain that ties me to old cycles, and surround me with people and patterns that point me closer to You.

Amen.

Reflection / Call to Action:

What "familiar" pattern keeps pulling me back into dysfunction?

_____

_____

_____

_____

_____

How can I choose freedom in my words, my boundaries, or my relationships this week?

_____

_____

_____

_____

_____

One cycle I'm breaking today and a declaration of God's

promise of freedom over it:

_____

_____

_____

_____

_____

_____

_____

_____

_____

_____

_____

_____

_____

_____

Day 15

Walking in Your New Name

"Anyone who belongs to Christ has become a new person. The old

life is gone; a new life has begun!"

2 Corinthians 5:17 (NLT)

Sis, freedom isn't just leaving something behind—

it's stepping into who you really are.

When you break cycles and choose freedom, the enemy will still try to whisper old names: unworthy, broken, difficult, too much, not enough. He'll use family, friends, or even your own doubts to make you question if you really deserve the life God is calling you into.

But here's the truth, you are not who you were in the cycle. You are not defined by dysfunction. You are not bound to your past. When God sets you free, He calls you forward. That means you don't just survive, you transform.

Think about Jacob in the Bible. His name meant "deceiver," but after wrestling with God, he walked away with a limp and a new name Israel, which means "God fights." That's what healing looks like. You may walk with some scars, but those scars carry a testimony of who God is in your life.

Sis, don't answer to old labels anymore. Don't shrink to fit back into places God already called you out of. Your freedom isn't just for you, it's proof that God still rewrites stories.

Lord,

Thank You for giving me a new name and a new life in You. Help me walk boldly in freedom, without fear of the old labels or chains. Remind me daily that my scars are proof of Your grace, not my shame.

Amen.

Reflection / Call to Action:

What old labels or names do I need to stop answering to?

_____

_____

_____

_____

_____

How has God already shown me glimpses of my "new

name?"

_____

_____

_____

_____

_____

A declaration of who I am now: (I will speak it over myself

this week).

_____

_____

_____

_____

_____

_____

_____

_____

_____

_____

_____

_____

_____

_____

Day 16

I'm Not for Everybody

"Obviously, I'm not trying to win the approval of people, but of

God. If pleasing people were my goal,

I would not be Christ's servant."

Galatians 1:10 (NLT)

Sis, stop shrinking to fit places you've outgrown.

I always say, *"I ain't for everybody,"* and that's the truth. For too long I exhausted myself trying to win approval from family, friends, even people who were never rooting for me in the first place. But freedom came when I realized that God didn't call me to be palatable, He called me to be purposeful.

Here's the thing, when you start living authentically, not everyone will clap. Some will misunderstand you. Some will mislabel you. Some will even resent the glow that came from God's hand on your life. And that's okay. Because Sis, peace comes when you finally accept that their opinion isn't your assignment.

Boundaries matter here too. Protecting your time, energy, and your heart is holy work. That looks like saying no without guilt, not overexplaining, and walking away when peace costs too much to stay.

Lord,

Remind me that I'm called to please You, not people. Give me the courage to stand firm in who I am and the wisdom to protect my peace with healthy boundaries.

Amen.

Reflection / Call to Action:

Where am I still trying to fit where I longer belong?

_____

_____

_____

_____

_____

What boundary do I need to set this week?

_____

_____

_____

_____

_____

One area where I'm ready to stop explaining myself and live authentically:

_____

_____

_____

_____

_____

_____

_____

_____

_____

_____

_____

_____

_____

_____

Day 17

Rediscovering You

"…Don't be dejected and sad, for the joy of the Lord

is your strength!"

Nehemiah 8:10 (NLT)

When you stop losing yourself in others, you

finally find yourself in God—and in the skin you're in.

Sis, let's be real. Sometimes you lose yourself in the name of love, loyalty, or just survival. You shrink so others can shine. You silence yourself so others can stay comfortable. You put your dreams on the shelf because you're too busy carrying everyone else's.

But when God breaks you free, something beautiful happens—you get to reintroduce yourself to yourself. Not the broken you. Not the silenced you. The real you—bold, radiant, and whole. And here's the truth: rediscovering you isn't just about prayer and journaling (though those are powerful). Healing is holistic. That means tending to your spirit, your body, and your mind.

Go to the gym. Clean up your eating. Watch how much more you love the body God gave you when you fuel it right.

Get your nails done, a fresh pedicure, your hair done, your face beat—remind yourself that you're worth the investment.

Take the spa day. Book the trip. Put yourself in spaces that refill your joy instead of draining it. And don't you dare feel guilty about it! Self-care isn't vanity—it's stewardship. When you care for yourself, you're saying to God: "I honor the masterpiece You created."

At first, rediscovery feels awkward. You'll ask: "What do I even like anymore? Who am I outside of the pain?" But piece by piece, God restores you until one day you catch yourself smiling in the mirror and whisper: "Oh, there she is."

Sis, real joy isn't in people, positions, or perfection. It's in God. And when His joy becomes your strength, the glow hits different—the healed glow, the healthy glow, the "I love myself enough to care for myself" glow. And nothing can steal that —no man, no drama, no past

Lord,

Thank You for restoring my joy and teaching me to care for myself again. Show me how to honor You with my body, my time, and my peace. Let my self-care be an act of worship that reflects the wholeness You've given me.

Amen.

Reflection / Call to Action:

One way I can prioritize self-care this week (A workout, a pedicure, a quiet day with God, etc.)

_____

_____

_____

_____

_____

Where have I put myself last? How can I flip that script?

_____

_____

_____

_____

_____

One self-care rhythm I'll commit to as part of my healing

journey:

_____

_____

_____

_____

_____

_____

_____

_____

_____

_____

_____

_____

_____

Day 18

Wholeness Is the Goal

"I pray that God, the source of hope, will fill you completely with joy and peace because you trust in him. Then you will overflow with confident hope through the power of the Holy Spirit."

Romans 15:13 (NLT)

Peace is good. Wholeness is better.

A turning point in my journey came after a hard conversation with my friend Kelly. In her honest way she said, "If you don't want to be in this place anymore, then make a decision and do something about it." That pierced me—but it was the truth I needed.

Not long after, I reflected publicly about how I didn't want to stay stuck mentally, physically, or spiritually. And Sis, once I made the choice, God honored it. Since then, I've found my stride. For every person I lost or had to release, He replaced them with stronger connections or deepened the ones He intended. My time, energy, and my home—my safe space—are now focused where they need to be.

Wholeness meant more than setting boundaries. It meant working on my health, investing in self-care, and surrounding myself with people who pour into me as much as I pour into them. It's not selfish—it's stewardship. You can't pour from an empty cup, and God never asked you to.

Lord,

Thank You for surrounding me with truth-tellers and prayer warriors. Thank You for reminding me that healing is a decision and wholeness is Your promise. Fill me with joy, peace, and hope as I continue to walk in alignment with You.

Amen.

Reflection / Call to Action:

What area of my life—mental, physical, or spiritual—

needs the most attention right now?

_____

_____

_____

_____

_____

Who in my circle helps push me toward wholeness?

_____

_____

_____

_____

_____

One action today that aligns with healing my whole self, not just one part.

_____

_____

_____

_____

_____

_____

_____

_____

_____

_____

_____

_____

_____

_____

Day 19

Protecting Your Peace

"Guard your heart above all else, for it determines the course of your

life."

Proverbs 4:23 (NLT)

What you allow in your space will either protect your peace or poison it.

Sis, healing isn't just about what you *walk away from*, it's also about what you *protect moving forward*. You can't pray for peace and entertain chaos. You can't ask God for wholeness and then give people unlimited access to drain you. This is where boundaries graduate to lifestyle.

Protecting your peace means being intentional about who and what you allow in your circle. It means not explaining why someone no longer has access, because your peace is reason enough. It means turning down invitations that don't align, walking away from toxic conversations, and sometimes closing the door on people you still love, but can't let disrupt your healing.

And let's be clear, protecting your peace isn't passive. It's active stewardship. That looks like:

✦ Keeping your home a safe place.

✦ Watching what you consume—TV, social media, music, conversations.

✦ Being mindful of your health—because when your

body is stressed, your spirit feels it too.

✦ Saying "no" and letting that be a complete sentence. Peace isn't something you stumble into—it's something you guard, pray over, and cultivate daily.

Lord,

      Teach me to guard my heart and protect my peace. Give me discernment to recognize what threatens it, courage to set boundaries, and wisdom to create an environment where Your presence thrives.

      Amen.

Reflection / Call to Action:

What drains my peace most right now—and what

boundary could protect me from it?

_____

_____

_____

_____

_____

How can I make my home or space more peaceful this

week?

_____

_____

_____

_____

_____

Post this declaration somewhere you will see it daily: "My peace is not negotiable." (My favorite place is my bathroom mirror). Write a few other declarations:

_____

_____

_____

_____

_____

_____

_____

_____

_____

_____

_____

_____

Day 20

Walking in Purpose

"For we are God's masterpiece. He has created us anew in Christ

Jesus, so we can do the good things he planned for us long ago."

Ephesians 2:10 (NLT)

Healing prepares you. Purpose propels you.

Sis, healing was never the destination, it was preparation. God didn't bring you through cycles, pain, and pruning just for you to survive—He was shaping you so you could thrive in the assignment He had waiting.

And purpose doesn't always look like a pulpit, a stage, or a spotlight. Sometimes it's simply showing up every day as the encourager, the truth-teller, the voice that helps people laugh through pain or find perspective in their mess. For me, it looks like the daily encouragements I share in the mornings, or my "nighty nite" posts that remind folks to rest while laughing at the petty things life throws at us. It may seem small, but it matters because encouragement is ministry, too.

Sis, don't miss this: purpose isn't always wrapped in titles. It's in your obedience to use *your* gift, whether that's writing, serving, teaching, creating, parenting, leading, or simply uplifting someone who thought they couldn't make it one more day. God designed you to reflect Him in your own unique lane.

When you've healed, walking in purpose feels lighter because you're no longer striving for approval. You're just flowing in who God made you to be: whole, free, and unapologetically you.

Lord,

Thank You for reminding me that my purpose doesn't have to look like anyone else's. Help me walk boldly in the assignment You've placed in my hands, whether through encouragement, humor, or showing up authentically. Let my life point others back to You.

Amen.

In what ways has healing prepared me for the purpose
God is calling me to now?

_____

_____

_____

_____

_____

What gifts or everyday actions (big or small) do I
carry that could serve as ministry to others?

_____

_____

_____

_____

_____

Where in my life do I need to stop striving for approval
and simply walk freely in who God created me to be?

_____

_____

_____

_____

_____

_____

_____

_____

_____

_____

_____

_____

_____

_____

Day 21

Everyday Ministry

"So encourage each other and build each other up, just as you are

already doing."

1 Thessalonians 5:11 (NLT)

You don't need a pulpit to preach—your life and your words are already a sermon.

Sis, let me tell you something: I don't stand in pulpits. That's not my lane. But every morning when I hit "post" on a word of encouragement, or every night when I drop my little "nighty nite, keep it real" reflections, that's ministry. Because ministry isn't about a microphone—it's about impact.

Sometimes folks think they need a title, a collar, or a platform to be used by God. But the truth? God uses regular, everyday people in regular, everyday ways. He uses your testimony in the grocery store line. He uses your story at work when somebody is quietly fighting battles nobody sees. He even uses your laughter—yes, even the "petty" humor that makes people exhale when life gets too heavy.

Encouragement is holy work. Speaking life into somebody's weary spirit is kingdom work. And if God has given you a voice, a testimony, or even just the courage to say, "Hey, I've been there too"—then Sis, you're already in ministry.

Don't underestimate how your daily obedience—your posts, your prayers, and your presence plants seeds you may never see grow. Somebody is healing, smiling, or holding on because you decided to show up authentically. That's purpose.

Lord,

Thank You for reminding me that ministry isn't about a platform—it's about people. Use my words, my story, and even my humor to point others back to You. Let my everyday life be a reflection of Your love.

Amen.

Reflection / Call to Action:

Who in my life is waiting on the encouragement only I can give?

_____

_____

_____

_____

_____

One small way I can be "everyday ministry" this week—through a post, a call, or even a smile.

_____

_____

_____

_____

_____

God used someone else's ordinary words to minister to

me when:

_____

_____

_____

_____

_____

_____

_____

_____

_____

_____

_____

_____

_____

_____

_____

Day 22

Choosing Joy on Purpose

"This is the day the Lord has made.

We will rejoice and be glad in it."

Psalm 118:24 (NLT)

Joy isn't found—it's chosen.

Sis, here's the truth—life is always going to give you reasons to be bitter, anxious, or weighed down. But joy? Joy is a choice. Joy is resistance. Joy is saying, "No matter what's happening around me, I refuse to let it steal what God put inside me."

Choosing joy doesn't mean pretending everything's perfect. It means shifting your focus. It's laughing even when life tried to break you. It's finding gratitude in small things—your morning coffee, a text from a friend, your child's smile—even when big things are unsettled.

Joy comes from perspective. Some of what stressed you last year, you don't even remember now. That's proof that storms pass, and joy outlasts them. So why not choose joy today instead of waiting until "things get better?" Protecting your peace set the foundation, but choosing joy builds the house. When you live in joy, you don't just survive—you thrive. And that joy becomes contagious. Your light encourages others to find theirs.

Lord,

Thank You for giving me joy that this world can't take away. Help me to choose joy on purpose each day, no matter what circumstances look like. Let my joy be strength and my smile be a testimony.

Amen.

Reflection / Call to Action:

One small thing I can be genuinely grateful for today:

_____

_____

_____

_____

_____

Where have I been waiting for things to "get better"

before I allow myself to feel joy?

_____

_____

_____

_____

_____

Three joy-bringers I can keep close (music, prayer, laughter, exercise, etc.) and use them this week.

_____

_____

_____

_____

_____

_____

_____

_____

_____

_____

_____

_____

_____

_____

Day 23

Releasing the Replay

"Don't let the sun go down while you are still angry, for anger gives

a foothold to the devil."

Ephesians 4:26–27 (NLT)

Sis, stop renting out space in your head for

arguments that are already over.

Let me keep it all the way real—I've laid in bed replaying arguments, mad at myself for not getting the right jab in. Running back the scene like I'm gonna rewrite history with the perfect comeback. But seriously—where's the joy in that?

Every replay is a thief. It robs your peace, steals your sleep, and drains your energy. Meanwhile, the person you're replaying? They're snoring, scrolling, or sipping on something without a care in the world. Sis, don't let somebody who ain't even thinking about you, live rent-free in your head.

Release is power. It's saying, "I could clap back, but my peace is too expensive. I could stew, but my joy is worth more." Let God handle it. Your silence, your growth, your glow—those are your best responses.

So tonight? Put the replay on mute. Roll over, pray, and rest. Because peace hits different when you choose it over pettiness.

Lord,

Free me from the trap of replaying what I can't change. Remind me that protecting my peace is better than proving my point. Teach me to trust You with the battles that don't deserve my energy.

Amen.

Reflection / Call to Action:

What argument have I been replaying that I need to

finally mute?

_____

_____

_____

_____

_____

I chose silence, prayer, or letting go instead of clapping

back and that choice affected my peace and growth how:

_____

_____

_____

_____

_____

What does it look like for me to trust God with battles that don't deserve my energy? How can I practice that trust daily?

_____

_____

_____

_____

_____

_____

_____

_____

_____

_____

_____

_____

_____

_____

Day 24

Making Room for What's Next

"For everything there is a season, a time for every activity under

heaven."

Ecclesiastes 3:1 (NLT)

Sis, you can't step into your next if your hands,

heart, and house are still cluttered with yesterday.

Let's be real—sometimes you say you're ready for God to move, but you're still holding on to old stuff, old people, and old patterns that have no place in where He's taking you. You can't receive new blessings when your arms are full of expired baggage.

Think about it: when you clean out a closet, you suddenly see space you didn't know you had. Same with your spirit. When you release what's broken, toxic, or simply outlived its season, you make room for joy, peace, and opportunities that fit the new you.

Making room might look like:

Decluttering your home so it truly feels like your safe place.

Releasing relationships that drain you more than they feed you.

Resetting your routines—trading chaos for order, distractions for discipline.

It's not just about letting go—it's about preparing. God is not sloppy. He's not going to pour new wine into old wineskins. He's waiting for you to clear the space so He can fill it with more than you imagined.

Lord,

Help me release what no longer serves me or honors You. Give me courage to let go, faith to trust Your timing, and vision to prepare for the next season You're bringing.

Amen.

Reflection / Call to Action:

What "expired baggage" is taking up space in my life

right now?

Three things I can release this week to create room for

new blessings:

One tangible step I can make: clean a space, end a

draining habit, or reset a routine.

_____

_____

_____

_____

_____

_____

_____

_____

_____

_____

_____

_____

_____

_____

Day 25

Embracing the Season You're In

"For everything there is a season, a time for every activity under

heaven."

Ecclesiastes 3:1 (NLT)

Peace comes when you stop fighting the season

you're in and start trusting the One who placed you in it.

Sis, let's be real—some seasons feel like overflow and others feel like drought. Some are full of answered prayers, and others are filled with waiting that seems to last forever. But here's the truth: every season has purpose, even the ones that don't feel good.

I used to waste so much energy rushing to the "next" that I missed the blessing in the "now." Lying in bed replaying arguments, worrying about who left, or stressing over why it hasn't happened yet, none of that produced joy. All it did was drain me, but God started teaching me: the same way nature doesn't skip from winter to summer without spring, I can't skip the process He's using to grow me. Each season is shaping me for what's next.

🌱 Waiting seasons grow patience.

🔥 Testing seasons refine character.

🌸 Harvest seasons teach gratitude.

When you embrace where you are instead of fighting it, you find peace—even in the unknown. And Sis, here's the good part: God is faithful in every season. He's not just the God of your breakthroughs—He's the God of your in-betweens too.

Lord,

Help me to stop fighting the season I'm in. Teach me to trust Your timing and find joy in the process. Give me peace in the waiting, strength in the testing, and gratitude in the harvest.

Amen.

Reflection / Call to Action:

What season do I think I'm in right now: waiting, testing, or harvest?

_____

_____

_____

_____

_____

How has God already shown up in this season (even in small ways)?

_____

_____

_____

_____

_____

I thank God for this lesson I believe God is teaching me in this season:

_____

_____

_____

_____

_____

_____

_____

_____

_____

_____

_____

_____

_____

_____

_____

_____

Day 26

Don't Rush the Process

"So be truly glad. There is wonderful joy ahead, even though you

must endure many trials for a little while."

1 Peter 1:6 (NLT)

The process may be painful, but it's also purposeful.

Sis, let me be honest with you—nobody likes the testing seasons. They stretch you, prune you, and pull things out of you that you didn't even know were there. But it was in those testing seasons that I learned how to *really* fast and pray. And if you've never tried it—whew, the clarity and the ability to hear God's voice is surreal.

I used to pray in frustration, asking, *"Lord, when will this be over?"* But fasting taught me a deeper prayer: *"Lord, what are You showing me in this?"* That shift changed everything. Instead of rushing past the hard part, I started sitting with it—trusting that God was doing something in me that comfort couldn't.

Growth doesn't come in the easy seasons. It comes in pressing, pruning, and refining. And though it feels heavy, don't miss this—God never wastes the process. Every tear, prayer, and sacrifice is shaping you into someone stronger, wiser, and more prepared for the promise ahead. So Sis, don't rush it. What you learn in this season will be the foundation for the next.

Lord,

Help me stop running from the process. Teach me to lean into prayer and fasting so I can clearly hear Your voice. Remind me that every trial has purpose and that You are shaping me for greater.

Amen.

Reflection / Call to Action:

Where have I been trying to "rush out" of the season I'm currently in?

_____

_____

_____

_____

_____

Have I considered fasting as part of my healing journey? One area (food, social media, distractions) I will lay down and use as a time for prayer this week.

_____

_____

_____

_____

_____

This is one way that God has matured me through a difficult process:

_____

_____

_____

_____

_____

_____

_____

_____

_____

_____

_____

_____

_____

_____

_____

_____

Day 27

Clarity After the Storm

"When the storms of life come, the wicked are whirled away, but the

godly have a lasting foundation."

Proverbs 10:25 (NLT)

The storm may shake you, but it will also sharpen your vision.

Sis, if you've ever come out of a hard season, you know that clarity hits different on the other side of the storm. What used to confuse you suddenly makes sense. What you thought you couldn't live without, you now see was only weighing you down.

Some of my clearest moments with God came after nights of crying, days of fasting, and seasons of feeling stripped bare. The storm felt cruel at the time, but it cleared the clutter I didn't have the strength to remove on my own. Clarity after the storm looks like:

Knowing who your real people are.

Seeing which doors God shut for your protection, not rejection.

Recognizing that peace is priceless and anything that costs you peace is too expensive.

Feeling lighter because you're no longer carrying what wasn't yours.

Here's the beauty—storms don't just reveal what was broken; they reveal how unshakable God's foundation really is. And once you see clearly, you can't unsee it. That's where wisdom, discernment, and peace are born.

Sis, don't despise the storm. Thank God for the clarity it leaves behind.

Lord,

Thank You for the storms that felt like they would take me out but instead taught me to see clearer. Help me walk in discernment and protect the clarity You've given me. Let me never go back to what You already cleared away.

Amen.

Reflection / Call to Action:

What storm has given me unexpected clarity?

_____

_____

_____

_____

_____

What people or things has God revealed to me don't

belong in my next season?

_____

_____

_____

_____

_____

Lessons I've learned from my most recent storm so I
don't forget when the next one comes:.

_____

_____

_____

_____

_____

_____

_____

_____

_____

_____

_____

_____

_____

Day 28

Resting in Clarity, Opening to Love

"Above all, clothe yourselves with love, which binds us all together in perfect harmony."

Colossians 3:14 (NLT)

Clarity clears the space. Love fills it.

Sis, storms strip away illusions, distractions, and dead weight. But after the storm? That's when you rest, breathe, and see clearly what (and who) truly matters. Resting in clarity doesn't mean you stop living—it means you stop striving. It means you're no longer chasing validation, replaying arguments, or trying to prove your worth. You've already learned: you are worth it. Period. And here's the shift, once you're settled in that truth, your heart is finally safe enough to open again. Not from desperation or loneliness, but from clarity and fullness. From knowing the kind of love you deserve.

Opening yourself to love again isn't weakness—it's faith that God heals. Faith that joy still exists. Faith that He can send someone who won't compete with your peace, but will complement it. So Sis, rest in your clarity. Guard your heart, yes, but don't lock it away. You deserve to love and be loved, not just in theory, but in action. God didn't bring you this far to leave you hardened. He brought you through the storm to show you that real love: healthy,

godly, lasting love, is still possible.

Lord,

Thank You for the clarity You've given me after my storms. Teach me how to rest in Your peace and open my heart again—not from fear, but from faith. Prepare me to both give and receive love in a way that honors You.

Amen.

Reflection / Call to Action:

Where in my life am I still guarded out of fear rather than wisdom?

_____

_____

_____

_____

_____

What does "being loved well" look like for me now that I've grown?

_____

_____

_____

_____

_____

A prayer asking God to prepare both my heart and the heart of the one He may be sending into my life:

_____

_____

_____

_____

_____

_____

_____

_____

_____

_____

_____

_____

_____

_____

_____

Day 29

Signs You're Ready for Love Again

"Guard your heart above all else,

for it determines the course of your life."

Proverbs 4:23 (NLT)

Healing makes you ready. Clarity keeps you steady.

Sis, let's be real: not every healed season means you're ready for love again. Sometimes God keeps you in a space of just Him + you a little longer. But there *are* signs that you've grown enough to welcome someone new—and not sabotage it. Here are a few ways you know you're ready for love again:

❖ **You're not bitter, —just wiser.** The thought of your past doesn't make you rage or spiral. It makes you grateful for the lessons and clear on what you won't repeat.

❖ **You like your own company.** You don't need someone to "complete" you. You're content, but you're open to being complemented.

❖ **Your boundaries are firm but healthy.** You don't over-explain, over-apologize, or accept red flags just to avoid being alone.

❖ **You're clear on your values.** You know what kind of partnership you want, and you're unwilling to settle for less than alignment with God's best.

✦ **You're not rushing.** Love will find you in peace, not panic. You're prepared to wait for God's timing instead of forcing what isn't right.

Being ready for love again doesn't mean you're flawless, it means you've healed enough to love without bleeding on someone else. It means you can receive love without suspicion and give it without losing yourself.

Sis, readiness isn't about having the perfect glow-up. It's about being whole enough to recognize when someone sees, values, and honors who you really are.

Lord,

Thank You for preparing my heart for healthy love. Remove any lingering fear or residue of the past, and make me ready to give and receive love in alignment with Your will.

Amen.

Reflection / Call to Action:

Which of these signs do I see in myself right now?

_____

_____

_____

_____

_____

Where might I need healing before love enters again?

_____

_____

_____

_____

_____

Three non-negotiables that will guide how I accept love

moving forward:

_____

_____

_____

_____

_____

_____

_____

_____

_____

_____

_____

_____

_____

Day 30

Breaking the Cycle for Good

"As a dog returns to its vomit, so a fool repeats his foolishness."

Proverbs 26:11 (NLT)

Discernment is knowing the difference. Healing is refusing to go back.

Sis, let me be transparent. I had a brief entanglement that went against everything I had just been delivered from. And the moment I saw it for what it was, red flags dressed in familiarity, I blocked, deleted, and put them on DND so fast it would make your head spin.

Why? Because why would I allow myself to fall for the same abusive cycle all over again? That's not growth. That's bondage. And God didn't free me to go running back to the very chains He just broke.

Here's the truth: the enemy doesn't always come at you with brand-new tricks. He often comes back with a "refreshed version" of what you already survived—just to see if you're really healed. But Sis, this time you know better. This time you see it earlier. This time you cut it off before it takes root.

Breaking cycles for good means choosing yourself, your peace, and your healing every single time—even when loneliness whispers, even when old habits try to creep back in. It means being so committed to your freedom that anything that smells like bondage doesn't get a second chance. And when you do that? That's when you know you're really ready for the love God does have for you. Because you've proven to yourself, and to the enemy, that you won't trade your healing for counterfeit affection.

Lord,

Thank You for giving me the wisdom to recognize cycles and the strength to walk away from them. Help me to never return to what You've freed me from. Prepare me for the love that aligns with Your will.

Amen.

Reflection / Call to Action:

What cycle has tried to creep back into my life recently?

_____

_____

_____

_____

_____

How can I remind myself that I'm not going back?

_____

_____

_____

_____

_____

A declaration of freedom I will speak over myself daily.

(e.g., "I won't return to cycles God delivered me from.")

_____

_____

_____

_____

_____

_____

_____

_____

_____

_____

_____

_____

Day 31

God's Timing in Love

"Yet the Lord longs to be gracious to you; therefore He will rise up

to show you compassion. For the Lord is a faithful God. Blessed

are those who wait for His help."

Isaiah 30:18 (NLT)

Sis, even the dreams you scribble down in "what if" moments aren't wasted. God can turn them into destiny.

Over four years ago, my therapist gave me a challenge. She said, "If you could describe the kind of man you'd want by your side in a perfect world, what would he be like?" At first, it felt silly—almost like daydreaming. But I took the exercise seriously and wrote this list:

- God is first in his life

- Loves his mother

- Treats daughters well

- Loves children

- Community service oriented

- Honest

- Respectful

- A good listener

At the time, it wasn't a prayer list. It wasn't me saying, "Lord, send me this tomorrow." It was just me putting on paper what I thought would reflect the kind of partner I'd want if I could choose. But here's the thing, God took that "perfect world" list and said, *"Daughter, I can do better than your imagination. I'll align this with My timing."*

Of course, before I could see it, I had to survive the *opposite* of it. I had to walk away from cycles of pain, betrayal, and manipulation. I had to learn what love wasn't, so I'd recognize what love truly is. Looking back, I see how God honored that little list. The man I love today reflects it—not because he's flawless, but because he's aligned with God. He doesn't compete with my calling, he complements it. He doesn't resent my light, he protects it. He doesn't drain me, he pours into me.

And the best part? My children get to witness this. My son gets to grow up seeing what steady, God-centered love looks like. My daughter isn't close enough yet to see it with her own eyes, but one day I pray she will. This isn't just about me finding love, it's about breaking cycles and about showing them that real love doesn't wound or diminish, but covers, protects, and lifts.

That's the legacy I want to leave, proof that God's timing is worth the wait, and that love aligned with Him is worth every heartbreak it took to get here.

Lord,

Thank You for turning even my "what if" dreams into answered prayers. Thank You for teaching me through the wrong love so I'd be ready for the right one. Help me steward this blessing well and model healthy, God-centered love for the ones watching me.

Amen.

Reflection / Call to Action:

If I write my "perfect world" list today, it will include:

_____

_____

_____

_____

_____

How has God used past pain to prepare me for the love I

deserve?

_____

_____

_____

_____

_____

Write this declaration: *"The love I receive will be the love that breaks cycles and leaves legacy."*

_____

_____

_____

_____

_____

_____

_____

_____

_____

_____

_____

_____

_____

_____

Bonus Day

Walking in the Love You Prayed For

"Two people are better off than one, for they can help each other succeed. If one person falls, the other can reach out and help. But someone who falls alone is in real trouble."

Ecclesiastes 4:9-10 (NLT)

Surviving prepared you. Healing equipped you. But Sis, walking in love again requires trust.

Let's be real—after surviving broken relationships, abuse, or betrayal, receiving healthy love can feel strange. You're so used to guarding yourself that when kindness shows up, you second-guess it. When consistency comes, you wait for the catch. When peace enters the room, you mistake it for boring. Sis, don't let survival mode rob you of what you prayed for. This is what healing was preparing you to receive.

Healthy love won't trigger your anxiety—it will calm it. Healthy love won't dim your light—it will shield it. Healthy love won't demand you shrink—it will celebrate your fullness. Here's what it looks like to walk in the love God gave you:

✦ Loosen your grip on control. Stop waiting for the other shoe to drop. Trust God enough to rest in the blessing He placed in your life.

✦ Be vulnerable again. Yes, it's scary. But true intimacy requires openness. Share your fears, dreams, and flaws.

✦ Match energy with energy. If he pours, you pour. If

he prays, you pray. Love grows when both people sow into it.

✦ Keep God at the center. Pray together, serve together, worship together—make Him the glue.

Walking in love after heartbreak is an act of faith. You're telling God, *"I trust You enough to open my heart again, and I trust this person enough to hold it."* And let me say this: you deserve to enjoy it. Don't sabotage what God sent by living in yesterday's shadows. Love doesn't always hurt—sometimes it heals.

Lord,

Thank You for preparing me for a love that reflects Your heart. Help me release fear, trust Your timing, and walk boldly in this blessing. Teach me to nurture this love with wisdom, joy, and faith.

Amen.

Reflection / Call to Action:

What fears from past relationships try to creep up when I think about loving again?

_____

_____

_____

_____

_____

How can I invite God into my relationship daily?

_____

_____

_____

_____

_____

One way I will intentionally pour back into someone who pours into me:

_____

_____

_____

_____

_____

_____

_____

_____

_____

_____

_____

_____

_____

_____

Epilogue – Sis, Keep Going

If you've made it here, sis, then you've walked with me through the raw, the messy, the painful, and the beautiful. You've heard my heart, my truth, and my tea. I need you to know that if God could bring me out, He can bring you out too.

This isn't just my story. This is a mirror for every woman who has been silenced, shamed, overlooked, or underestimated. Every woman who thought survival was all she'd get. Every woman who prayed in the dark wondering if God was even listening. He was, He is, And He always will be.

You may still be in your "Day 1," feeling like that little girl who just wants to be safe. Or maybe you're somewhere in the middle, fighting through the tears and wrestling with forgiveness. Or maybe, like me, you're standing in a new season that feels lighter, freer, softer. — You're finally breathing without the weight of old chains.

Wherever you are, hear me: don't stop here. Healing is a journey, not a destination. Keep talking to God. Keep setting boundaries. Keep walking away from what doesn't honor you. Keep holding out for the love and life you deserve.

Sis, the world needs your healed voice, your healed vision, your healed leadership. Don't shrink. Don't dim. Don't apologize for your glow. If you ever forget? Come reread these pages. Let them remind you that you are living proof of God's grace, resilience, and restoration. Now go shine. Go lead. Go love. Go be the woman God always knew you'd become. And remember, you're never alone.

With love & truth,

Dr. B

My Prayer for You

Lord,

Thank You for never leaving us, even in moments we felt most abandoned. Thank You for rewriting our story and reminding us that healing is possible.

For the sister reading this, I ask that You meet her right where she is and whisper to her spirit: *"You are loved, you are chosen, you are free."*

Amen.

FINAL WORD

"And I am certain that God, who began the good work within you,

will continue his work until it is finally finished on the day when

Christ Jesus returns."

Philippians 1:6 (NLT)

Lord,

Thank You for walking with me through every valley, mountain, tear and breakthrough. I release the past, I embrace the present, and I trust You with my future. Seal the healing You've begun in me, and let my life be a testimony of Your faithfulness.

May I walk in love, strength, and wholeness until the day You complete the good work You started.

Amen.

Healed Life Vision Statement

Sis, healing is not the end of your story, it's the beginning of a new one. You've survived the breaking, you've walked through the wilderness, and you've chosen wholeness. Now the question is: how will you live differently? What will you protect, prioritize, and pursue with the healed version of yourself?

Write your Healed Life Vision Statement. Include how you want to love, lead, parent, serve, and show up in the world. Be bold, be specific, and let it be your roadmap forward. Here is my Healed Life Vision Statement as an example:

I choose **peace over chaos.**

I choose **purpose over pain.**

I choose **love that covers me, honors me, and helps me show up better** for those I lead and those I love.

In this healed life, **God is always first.**

My family is covered.

My leadership flows from **empathy and strength, not survival and fear.**

I no longer shrink.

I no longer silence my truth.

I no longer stay in rooms where I am not respected.

I will **lead with clarity, love with courage, and protect my joy like it's sacred — because it is.**

This healed version of me will break **generational curses,** build **generational blessings,** and leave a legacy that says: *She answered God's way out, and she never looked back.*

My Healed Life Vision Statement:

_____

_____

_____

_____

_____

_____

_____

_____

_____

_____

_____

_____

_____

_____

_____

Sis, if you've walked with me through these 31 days, you already know this isn't just about pain, it's about purpose. I've shown you my scars, not to stay stuck in them, but to prove that God can turn even the ugliest chapters into a testimony worth sharing.

I didn't get here overnight. Healing was messy. Some days I cried, some days I wanted to quit altogether. But God. Every step, He was peeling back layers of brokenness and showing me I didn't have to live in survival mode anymore.

So this isn't goodbye. This is me passing you the baton. My story is mine, but your story is waiting to be written too. Pick up your pen, let God guide your hand, and write it in truth, love, and power.

Sis, the best is yet to come.

— Dr. B 🖤

www.ingramcontent.com/pod-product-compliance
Lightning Source LLC
Chambersburg PA
CBHW051822090426
42736CB00011B/1604